DEAD HORSES

Joan Colby

FUTURECYCLE PRESS
Mineral Bluff, Georgia

Copyright © 2012 Joan Colby
All Rights Reserved

Published by FutureCycle Press
Mineral Bluff, Georgia, USA

ISBN 978-1-938853-02-9

Contents

Dead Horses.. 7
Temple Horses at Tamil Nadu.. 9
Heartless.. 10
Founder.. 12
Barn Fire.. 14
Horsewoman.. 15
Witch.. 16
Farming.. 18
Country Burial.. 21
Requiem for a Farrier... 22
March 24.. 24
Bohemian Lodge... 26
Friday Night at the Dump... 28
Drought.. 30
Western Minnesota.. 32
Saddlesoap... 34
Roadkill.. 36
The Lunar Year... 38
Fences.. 42
Hammering... 44
Hayhook.. 45
Renovations.. 46
The Threshing Bee and Steam Show............................... 48
Pederson's.. 49
Ox Team at Garfield Farm.. 50
Two Deaths... 52

Acknowledgments... 57

For Alan and my Boat House friends

Dead Horses

Now that they are dead or gone, the dream
Is always of a field where running horses
Flash past, hooves catching and echoing light,
The grass lush, milkweed or Queen Anne's lace
Along the fencerows. Then suddenly it's winter,
Snow is falling, shapes are haloed, the sky is bleak.

You might awaken, amazed the sound of horses
Has passed, diminished just as a streak of daylight
Pours through the curtains, fills bastions of lace
As your eyes fill with sorrow recalling a winter
Where nothing ever thawed, each vista bleak.
You knew the vault of loss, the end of dreams,

But would not acknowledge it, that blight of light
Unraveling the seams of some grandmother's lace
Concoction that formed a history, that overwintered
In every house you slept in, every bleak
Ceiling that you woke to, emptying dreams
Into a landscape now bereft of horses.

Those horses: the dappled one like old lace
Fading into the slushy nouns of winter,
Its whites and blacks and greys as bleak
As a deserted park, no childhood dreams
Anchored by swingsets or gymnastic horses
On which you vaulted, slim and young and light

As any snowflake in any kind of winter,
The brilliant sled-filled one, even the bleak

Fog-frosted dawns, the ones that hid all dreams
Until they burst from the icy mists like horses
Racing to the barns in that first light
Presaging hunger, muzzles coated with the lace

Of their breathing, how they stormed the bleak
Hollows where your final splintered dreams
Corroded. You want them now, those horses
Crashing the earth with sound as if light
Had been surpassed by speed, as if the laces
That bind you to your bones gave way to winter's

Blast, unreining every dream, freeing the horses
Of your past, lightening that blanket of heavy lace
Until you open your arms to winter and everything holy or bleak.

Temple Horses at Tamil Nadu

Row upon row, alarmed with war paint
Or a ceremonial exuberance
Like tapers of the Holy Ghost, ears
Red as vigil lights. Sacred in any
Belief system, their ghee-colored faces
Echo the magistery of light,
Eyes popping in frozen ecstasy,
Assuming the grimace known as flehmen,
Distressed from colic or alert for sex.
In any event, nothing laughable
Occurs here or in any cathedral
Where deities sit in benediction,
Assume extraordinary positions,
Or hang in agony.

These horses do none of that.
Instead they stand
Silenced in stasis,
Formed of the clay
That invigorated the first man
Who rose naked in the perfect garden
To name these beasts that await
His last command, bridled and bedecked.

Heartless

Bull rider says "Young, I was
Pea-hearted, shot my
Appaloosa when he broke a
Pastern, without a qualm, kicked out
My first wife, that bitch.
Now I weep for my crippled
Aussie, ain't got the heart
To put him down. And my
Daughter I barely know
Down in Abilene."

I know. Drowned kittens,
Coons and possums trapped,
Coyotes shotgunned, the
Barncat staggering, frothing
After eating a poisoned crow.
Wearing heavy leather gloves,
We caught him concerned only
About rabies.

Now running a saline drip
Into the cat with failing
Kidneys. Hand-feeding sliced
London broil to the old
Dying hound. Carrying
Asian ladybugs outdoors, letting
Spiders spin, snakes sun,
Salamanders crawl about the wellhouse.

Young, I wrote
Poems as harsh and fierce
As ice on barbed wire, feared
Nothing more than sentiment,
A fatal softening like rot
In an onion or the lethal odor
Of cut flowers left too long.

It takes almost a lifetime to learn
Heartlessness is no armor at all.

Founder

When the horse dies,
The brain is last to succumb.
The thrashing legs stilled.
The twitching lip.
The eye shines onward
Desperate to live. I wait
For it to film.

Needle in the vein,
She goes down fast,
Not like a wall crumbling
In tutus of dust
But like a stricken tree, sudden,
Awful, loud.

Now at last
She lies peacefully,
Relaxed as she slept
When newborn,
Her dam standing sentry
In the ancient habit of mares.

Founder, that's a word
For horses and ships.
Coffin bones sinking and spars,
Deep-creaking agony
Of blood and ocean,
Common denominator of salt.
She licked salt blocks,
A bin of oats,

Bucket dark with water.
Once she raced like a schooner,
Hooves and sails flying,
Steel in her mouth,
A crowd shouting
Like a crew sighting land.

Her stall is empty now,
Lonesome bay of straw
Gilded with dust.

In winter in the stone barn,
She steamed
As if below decks.
In summer, manure smoked
As if alive, inoffensive waste
Of grass eaters, a holiness mad
Nebuchadnezzar hungered for.

Evolution made the horse
Pose upon landlocked toes
Like a ballet dancer. The hoof cannot expand.
Blood flows and flows,
Loosening anchors of laminae
Till like a ship broadsided in big seas
The horse rocks back
Sweating, its salted hide
Glazing eyes and grinding teeth
Like a keel sundering,
Is lost now, lost
To the renderer and his hooks.

Barn Fire

Green, dense, moist, packed and stacked
Ten high to fill the loft. A narrow aisle
Filters light lauded with dust.
A yeasty smell, good enough to eat
Or kindle. How the heat begins to smolder
Deep, deep within the wick of bale,
A thin snake of smoke like the contrail
Of a high-flying jet echoing
Its sound breaks. Swallow nests,
Then the great beams catch and glow. That's
How it starts, not a cigarette
Discarded or a wire gnawed by rats.
The provender ignites its own safekeeping.
Its axioms of immolation bless
The harvest with a baleful flame. Here's the rest
Of that story—that story
Of storage, of keeping safe, of keeping
Everything inviolate. Each story is a myth
In which someone discovers fire,
And then it all begins.

Horsewoman

She lost her eye
When Luck O the Roll
Kicked out suddenly
While being shod.

She had absently
Stepped behind him.
The barn aisle dim and dusty.

The farrier dropped
Pullers and hammers,
Shouted out loud.

Weeks in a coma,
Her husband felt
Impotent. Had to do something.
Had the horse put down.

The plastic surgeon
Restored a face
Not quite hers.

One good eye.
No taste. No smell.
But alive. Lucky.

She asks. He tells her.
That eye, offset, but saved,
Stares. And stares.
He's silent.

Witch

Leggy, incorrigible from the outset,
Whaling on her patient dam
Or sucking noisily. She cracked
Your sternum when you were
Tailing her as I drew blood.

Striking or wheeling for a kick,
She reared when the buyer came to look.
Breaking her, Pedro said, "She'll win
With this temper." That name.

When she hit the track,
The trainer shook his head. "She
Clears the shedrow when she comes down
The aisle." Shaking her nose chain
Like a castanet.

Bullet works in the morning,
That secular time when ecstasy
Did not roll her eyes.

Her first start, she flew so wide
She ran a mile or more in six furlongs.
The railbirds shrank into the stands,
Making a cross by her number.

Impertinent but cunning when she kindly took
Sugar from our hands, we locked on hope
Dashed in the afternoon
When the church of spectators prayed

And shouted in tongues over their tickets
And she went mad.

The music in her head
Clamored for her to dance,
To dwell or prop or buck—
Whatever a sorceress wants.

"A bolter," the stewards said.
Irascible in the gate,
A danger on the track. Maenad I birthed
That Easter morning. Ruled off

My dark and lovely
Filly with a snip.

Farming

One of the most dangerous occupations

Heaped with straw and manure steaming
In a January dawn, the spreader's load
Is half frozen, half smoldering
In its compacted heart. Unquenchable
Self-immolation. The icy boards groan.

His dream, at ten, to farm like his forebears.
I can handle it. His mother pouring coffee nods,
His father still showering for the day job
That keeps the old place going.

She hears the tractor chugging along the ditch
To the field of stubble hauling its burden.
After awhile, the silence seizes her,
The glazed window framing a frieze:
Rising sun glancing off yellow steel
Stalled at the margin of battered corn—
Rags twisting in the wind.

His boots plunge periods in crusted snow.
His heart, though, is a question mark.
He knows the answer before he gets there:
The shredded horror of his boy.
He wants to shout *How many times*
Have I told you. The old tractor
Hard to start. Just a moment to
Clear the blades. The cold. The wish

For the warm kitchen. The PTO churns
Implacably, spitting bits of sinew and yarn.

She lies in the darkened bedroom unable to attend
Wake or funeral, imagining the blame
In the neighbors' eyes. *Only 10—*
What were they thinking. 20 below—
An exaggeration but one that befits
A story of parents luxuriating
Over oatmeal while the boy
Struggled with jammed iron.
Her heart jams each time she thinks
Of how he must have shouted.

Later, she gets to her feet. This farm
Must go on. It's what the boy
Would want. His dream that was her dream.
She says *He died doing what he loved.*

He turns away. She wasn't at that scene
Of impossible destruction. She didn't have

To turn the key, to cradle
What was left. His footprints in the snow
So deeply implanted, he feels the freeze
Climb to his sternum and erupt
Like the spontaneous combustion of waste.

In that cold farmhouse,
A year later to the day,
He sits down in his easy chair,

The shotgun in his lap.
Now she'll have something to discover.

Vintage tales of hardship and survival:
Granddad crushed when the tractor toppled
On Brier Hill. How Uncle John lost his arm
To the picker. Samuel smothered
In the silo, lungs full of harvest.

She overlooks the acres
Awaiting disc and plow.
An early spring, she'll turn
That dark earth over.

Country Burial

Blacktop to gravel to dirt
That in another season will surely
Sink a procession such as this.
Then the rutted grassy trail
Past a lone stone, "Founded 1840,"

The square-cornered hole,
Old words of solace and hope.
Each hand armed with a yellow rose,
The final ammunition of love.

Five long-haired daughters weeping,
A poetic quintet to take the abstract view
Of an outsider here for duty's sake.

Acres of standing corn encircle this
Upheaval of leprous stones
With vanishing inscriptions.

The husband looks poleaxed,
Numb in his new suit
Bought for next month's planned
Renewal of vows.

Requiem for a Farrier

Me holding the shank of the demonic filly,
Her Medusa mane snaked with cockleburs,
While you grab her left fore to trim the hoof
That flies up as she rears and strikes,
Both of us dodging, me
Yanking the nose chain, you hollering
Let's get the sledgehammer and kill her.
We laughed about that later when,
Subdued with acepromazine, she stood
Still rolling her pearl-rimmed evil eye
Where your image hung.

The two of us working in tandem
To catch the halterless colt
Of the man who wouldn't pay you
And shag it into the trailer,
Rustlers grinning at the surprise
Of the outwitted. You trading for a mare
With rainrot, barren.

All your stories
Told over black coffee when the anvil
Pullers and hammers had been stored
In the back of the truck threatened
With repossession. You and a buddy
Shoeing a barnful for a rich industrialist
Famous for bad checks. You just smirked.
Only a day's work. Who cares.
I tell your fortune, turn
Over the Tarot card—the Hanged Man.

Three of us trying to load
Your mare and month-old filly
To haul to the farm where you bartered
Half the dam for a breeding.
The mare stamping and whinnying,
The filly galloping off down the road.
The van earthquaking.
You shrugged. *Tomorrow hangs*
Just over the earth's wheel.

Another of your money-making schemes,
The framed horseshoes
With an invented provenance of some famous racer,
Failed to find a market.
You didn't care. *Hang on. Things have to get better.*

After the landlord kicked you out,
Shoeing my big gelding, you mentioned
Bankruptcy, not much to lose.
Your voice hung on the half-thought,
That half-grin shifting your mustache.

The night your wife ran off,
The bashed wall, the bourbon.

March 24

Because you abhorred a mess.
Because you were always overly neat.
Shedrow swept and raked.
Flowers in boxes, pastures mowed.
Stalls limed and clean.

Because pain fit you like too-tight jeans.
Vicodin was constipating,
Whiskey obscene with vomit.

Because you could no longer do anything
You loved. The young colts unbroken.
The tractor rusting. Your wife
Carping about the money.
Or just because.

You walked down the lane to the gate,
Locked it behind you. Sat
On the roadside and carefully removed
All of your clothes and folded them
Before picking up the shotgun.

Now it's just speculation.
How you'd never wish to despoil
Your homestead.
How you hoped to embarrass
Your wife.
How your friends would finally see
How little you possessed.

How the bank, the doctors, the V.A.,
All the damn bureaucrats
Could no longer harass you.
How you came into the world naked
And would leave like that.

Bohemian Lodge

The best roast duck
Cloaked in orange,
Crisp as autumn.
Side dishes of pickled stuff.
Old Fashioneds with bitters.

An old-time roadhouse,
One old-time gangsters
Might have frequented.
Top level: a seedy motel.
Lower level strung with lights.
Bohemian glass and enamelware.

The bar dark wood, dark mirror.
Tables intimate, no AC, a scent of mold.
Secret passions, illicit adventures
Out on Highway 47.

The old folks, whose family photos,
Embroidered caps, and aprons
Decorated the foyer, died. A son
Took over. Drugs, dementia, altercations

With the cook, a madman,
Who took a cleaver to him.
Half the torso buried one place,
Arms another. The head and the rest
Never found.

Weeds overtake the walls
Of the Bohemian Lodge
That no one wants to buy or lease
Or even tear down.

Friday Night at the Dump

Headlights switched on,
A dozen or more feasting.
Fat black Friar Tucks
Tucking in. Heads down
In dumpsters tossing
Styrofoam and pizza cartons,
Jars of peanut butter, soup cans,
Cookies, pasta, a reddish mess.

Some climb in as if sinking
Into a hot tub. Round ears poke up
Wearing a McDonald's tray
Like a jaunty sailor's cap.

Half an acre of garbage
All the way to the jackpines.
A pair of cubs play
With a half-eaten doughnut.

We venture from our trucks
With plastic bags of more.
Satiated, smeared, oafish,
They barely look up.

Open dumpsters, split sacks,
Cavorting like a gross ballet,
Claws raking a display of waste.
The stench is bad.
The moon is up.

Come hunting season, rifles
Poke from 4 × 4s.
Lulled, the bears rise,
Jack-in-boxes, snouts glopped
With marshmallow gunk,
Their last supper.

Drought

The wells went dry, then the rivers
Lessened to a trickle and disappeared,
Leaving only indentations studded with pebbles
And the occasional boulder.

We sent the cattle to slaughter rather than watch them die of thirst.
Chickens scratched a pointless calligraphy in bare earth and ants
Caravanned through clapboards, not for sugar
But for water.

Now the water witch dances with his willow rod,
Comes up with nothing, his arms numb with loss.
Levels of everything diminish. Even tears
Clog in our ducts, leaving us red-eyed and sorry.

Our pockets, once jingling with hope,
Are full of sand. Scorpions
Crawl where the wisteria used to flower
Over the old pergola. Every afternoon
Clouds float over, empty as pillowcases.

Chac, god of rain, frowns on the Mayan virgins,
Throws his sacks of water over his shoulder and stomps off.
Their bones in the empty wells mean nothing,
Mean less than nothing.
Lining up the constellations
Fails to help.

The dust storms drive everyone to the sea
Where the pickings are slim, the water
Murderous. On the weather maps,
A fiery splotch promises more of the same.

What can we give each other
Besides the names of every kind of water
Into which we ever dipped our hands—
The Great Lakes, the springs, the creeks, the rivers—
And always the blessing of the rain.

Pay attention now. Look for one
Green thing to remember.

Western Minnesota

Balsams throng the river's edge,
Lovers of poverty, stark
And ascetic in black needles.

A communion of the faithful.
Thin soil, dark water.
Bristly nuns chanting plainsong.

Ice curdles the shoreline. Fractured
Slabs. Midstream the river
Runs freely, a cold snake.

A rounded barn crouches
On the far bank. Smoke plumes
From the farmhouse chimney.
This country
Is large and vacant.

Two hawks circle
A dull January sky. East of here,
The land flattens and pours
Like batter as far as you can see.
Anchored by occasional houses,
Its pretensions are of use
Not beauty. A woman in a door
Calls to a man on a tractor
Pushing snow
Into neat clumps like bumper crops

And a dog crosses
The road purposefully,
Carrying something dead.

Saddlesoap

Saddlesoaping leather,
Cracks inhaling, softening
Like kisses. Fingers work it in.

The bridle suspends
From a metal hanger
Like a frame or skeleton
Where energy is contained.

I unbuckle
Each of its parts,
Dismount the snaffle,
Its double rings too large
For an affianced finger.

Browband, martingale,
The reins loose and dangling
As the legs of prepubescent girls.

As if stuffed with monstrous cabbages,
His hard protuberant belly
Traps me against the tackroom wall.

Hands fingering my hair—*lovely
Auburn*—lips seeking, fingers. I
Struggle, duck, run into the stall.

My chestnut mare sways
Her haunches. Lustrous uncomprehending

Eyes. Arms around her neck, I tremble,
Our hearts beating together.

His footsteps, the stable door
Shutting.

My finger still greasy
With saddlesoap. The smell
Of new hay, manure.

The bit, polished steel.
A dulled sterling silences
What I will never speak.

Roadkill

Dead skunk on the road.
One hundred degrees, the stink is bad.
The county should be out
To scrape it up, but after two days
We take our shovels to it.

Traveling north, another skunk
Creased in the highway. Twin kittens
Pawing helplessly at her.
The kids beg us to stop.
We explain why not and drive on.

Everywhere are deer, muskrats,
Raccoons, possums, cats, even birds
Flying too low or alighting
On something already killed,

Blacktop littered as if
Figments of imagination
Had spun off to sizzle
Under a July sun.

Anesthetized, we hardly comprehend
What these clumps of fur and sinew were,
And we don't much care.

Not like the man, a week ago,
Who, seeing ducklings on the tollway,
Left his car running and rushed

To their rescue. He was hit
Almost at once, then hit again.

Roadkill. Today, a smear
Greyish, flattened. We keep going.

The Lunar Year

Hunger Moon

That's when the food ran out. The stock
Depleted, even the saved potatoes gone,
Rotten at the eyes. Our savings cleft
By half, all love foreclosed, the doors
Of home padlocked, the windows boarded.
What else can happen? Weather broods
Over the bleak horizon. This moon is also known
As the snow moon.

Crow Moon

The raven invented the world. Now the crow rules
Its lesser partitions. It encompasses
The slyness of politicians, the ruthlessness of love.
It waits for things to die or else it torments
Songbirds, those who can tongue
A harmony every crow despises.

Egg Moon

The lost wax process creates an egg
Of gorgeous dimensions, Byzantine
Geometrics suggesting a rage of contained
Passion. But another egg is pure.
Cool in the palm and distant
As that place where everything begins.

Milk Moon

It is this specialization that defines us.
How we link to every creature
That nurses its young. That
Baptismal drink the Orient refuses
After a certain age. What sort of wisdom
Clinks bottles on a stoop at dawn
Like earliest, beloved memories.

Strawberry Moon

You find them knitting the pasture
With rubies, the wild sort
Whose sweetness is so compact, so perfect
That cultivation seems a sort of sin,
Original as the path that led us out
Of infancy to the bloody-hearted world,
Wearing its seeds like a cloak.

Thunder Moon

Everything here depends on nitrogen
Of which thunder is merely the voice,
As a slap is the sound of forked anger,
The sound angels made as they fell
Into the firmament. The first denial.

Sturgeon Moon

Producers of caviar and isinglass,
One richly edible, the other a bonding agent

Like the lust that glues two lovers.
Flesh of temperate waters. The miracle
That feeds a jubilation
Of disbelievers. Cast your net. Have patience.

Barley Moon

All grains were once wild,
Uncultivated, there for the reaping,
There for the first lively spirits
Fermenting like every wish into
Something achievable, the malt
Of high ambition.

Harvest Moon

Every goddess walks
Under that parasol, her arms
A cornucopia of fulfillment.
No wonder we worship this
Unblemished guise. No wonder
We think no matter how many banks
Fail, how many ships break into pieces
In the coming gales, we'll still
Have this: how we were blessed
Just as the good times ended.

Hunter's Moon

That's what we do when everything
We counted on has collapsed
And all coffers are empty, all drawers

Divested of silk, all trigger fingers
Reinvested with darkness. Walk
Silently in the tracks of the dispossessed,
Ensuring it will not be you.

Cold Moon

Hunker down. Survival is now the key
To your heart, the tone-deaf song.
If you make a fire it is certain
To go out while you're asleep.
You'll wake with your feet frozen
In a crossroad of bad choices.
Shaking is the way your body
Fights cold like this. Huddle together.

Wolf Moon

They have come back, those predators
Of the prairie, the steppe, the open range,
Protected as a parliament
Of oligarchs, their guard hairs rising
As they sight you, out there
In your unarmed villages.

Fences

Auger corkscrewed through topsoil
The color of Grand Marnier, bored
Deeper into rich liquor where oak posts
Creosoted against rot were set
And tamped. Four boards properly
Nailed on the obverse side. Squared
And braced corners. Sixteen-foot
Pole gates hung.

Seeded in a mix of timothy and clover,
A cover crop of oats to shade growth.
They surveyed their toil. The horses
Thundered off the van and, heads down,
Divined the ritual of grazing.

Fenced and crossfenced, pastures switched
To rest and recover. Trodden dirt
By the stock tank graveled. Loose boards
Shored up. For years, side by side,
Pounding nails, repairing ravages of cribbers,
Leaners, butt rubbers, kickers,
Foals that slid under, racers that crashed
Or sailed. Those fences sturdy as biceps,
As homespun hearts, as presumed vigor.

After she went into the home and the horses
Were auctioned, he stood squarely
On his porch as if the loose
Skin of his jowls and upper arms

And the way his overalls hung
From his bones, as if he'd become
Insubstantial, were simply a figment
And the shadow he cast would cease
To lengthen like a runaway colt
Getting away from him as he watched
The fences, post and rail,
Come down.

Hammering

My neighbor has been roofing his barn
For the last several weeks,
Down to the bare beams,
Replacing the ruined wood.
His hammer ratchets the morning
Out of the sycamores. It's taking
Him too long, I think, a job
For more than one man. But he's
Industrious. I can see the sheets
Of plywood bright as toffee.
He's got the squares of shingles stacked.
Every night he stretches a blue tarp
Over his handiwork in case of rain.
Every daylight hour, I hear the knock
Of his nails arcing the planes,
And if I walk along the roadside thick
With chicory and wild carrot, I see him
Kneeling at noontide, his muscled forearm
Upraised, about to strike.

Hayhook

Grasp the baling twine and toss
To stack ten high in the dim loft,
Sweet alfalfa scent, green castles
Of good fodder. Sweat streams
Bare arms, dust triggers nerve ends,
A winter's worth stored.

Hayhook, rusted crescent
Workmanlike, forged, leather-gloved
Grip, how the heart requires
Necessities disguised as wants.

A January morning like any other.
Spread-legged in the loft door,
You hook a bale, and the hay hook
Curves around the twine
The way lovers twine in sleep.

So many times you've repeated
This simple motion. Today the hook
Reveals its obstinacy. It won't
Let go and you can't either.
The neural signal hooks itself
Into an arc of falling.

You lie prone on the concrete barn aisle,
Spread-eagled as a banished angel
Haloed in blood, the hook still
Frozen in your fist.

Renovations

When we open the wall,
An intricacy of wasps' nests
Like the ruins of Angkor Wat.

Long abandoned, the paper apartments
Collapse at a touch. It's surprising
What is found. The newspapers

Dated 1874 used for insulation
Crumbled to golden dust before
We could read a word.

It's like discovering a journal
You kept years ago. How naïve
You were, but in a way

Heart-breaking as only the young are
In their solemnities.
Or finding a letter you never answered,

And an inked calligraphy
Opens your spirit like an
Exotic bird call.

This is not restoration, this task,
Not duplication of
Historical details.

Instead, a new décor,
A room opening to
Another room for space and light

To see beyond
The papyrus cells
Of memory.

The Threshing Bee and Steam Show

Clam shell seats have bent them,
Sloped the shoulders shaping a posture:
Old farmer. Short sleeves, striped or plaid,
Pressed dungarees or dark work pants.
Scrawny, arms ropey with lean muscle,
Burnt with a thousand suns.
White-haired or grey, clean-shaven.
John Deere or Seed caps, Red Wing work shoes.

Average age of seventy-plus. Still farming,
Beans or corn. Winter wheat,
Milk cows or custom hay. How many seasons
In the fields astride the tractors
Pulling disc, plow, picker, mower, spreader.
Gripping the wheel, shifting gears,
Down the long rows sunup to sundown,
Cornering at the verge.

In winter barns, they restore
The ancient tractors—the 1940 Allis Chalmers,
The '31 Fordson, the '50 Harvester—
To a pristine condition.

Today, the old tractors shine.
In glossy paint, scrubbed tires, they parade,
The old farmers slumped at the wheels
Steering into applause, waving,
Some faintly smiling, others proudly stern
As if they were still young and tough and upright.

Pederson's

Udina Country Club is what we called it.
On the arrowhead where Route 20
Met Plank Road. A country tavern,
Workmen's lunches, burgers or chili,
Shot and a beer. Evenings, farmers
Gathered to talk corn yields or bean futures,
Weather always a hot topic.

The state decided to level it,
Fix the intersection for suburban sprawl
That collapsed with the housing market.
Traffic lights flash red and green,
Arrow us into t-squared turns
Instead of the old curves.

The cemetery is still there
Behind what was Pederson's,
Tombstones upraised as glasses
When the work was done.

Ox Team at Garfield Farm

Paired shortly after birth.
By two months bearing
The smallest yoke,
Learning the commands
Which nigh ox and off ox
Understand differently,
Always the same position,
Yoked or stalled.
Nigh ox to the right.
Off ox to the left.

Long horns intact
To keep the wooden yoke
In place. Controlled
By voice or motion.
Obedient and calm, their huge
Bodies compliant to plow,
Wagon, or log chain.

The ox driver points out
What fables those Westerns were:
Wagon trains circling
Their handsome horse hitches.

It was oxen
That opened the west,
Able to live on almost nothing,
To unmoor the mired cart,
Plod all day in patience.

No special breed, just
Cattle that were taught
To work. These two are ruddy
And boxlike with fleshy ivory nostrils
And the placid eyes of servants.
Each has one horntip screwed with brass.
Each has a name: Nigh Ox—Off Ox.

They think as an ensemble,
Mirror images of toil.
If one dies, the other is useless.

Two Deaths

I

The hurt owl
In the gravel roadway shifts
From one claw to the other,
The iris of one eye splattered
Like ink on yellow
Cellophane. The other eye
Stares, a perfect target,
Distrustful, woozy.
It has fluffed itself
Big as a tombstone: tufted
Earfeathers, scythe-beak clacking,
Its little tongue snake-pale.

II

The colt is still alive
On his feet, plodding, head down,
In slow circles, fur matted with sawdust,
Eye a prayer of flies.
Chainsawing dullness, legs buckle
Him down into a heap—
Swollen belly, head flung
At a distorted angle.
Last night, he thrashed in the stall
While you inoculated sleep.
A grey-white rat slid past
On a beam above your head, ghostlike.
I held the water bucket

To the colt's lips. You supported
Him as he drank shallowly,
Then sighed and rested
His head on a flake of straw.
Dawn gripped the edges of the window.
Mourning doves began to call.
The colt's sides heaved
And heaved and heaved. He went on breathing.

III

It will be another scorcher. Already, heat
Pleats the inner wrists of willow leaves
And, in the dips of pasture, mist
Is burning off.
You choke a rat
From the white cat's jaws,
A gift of sustenance for the owl
Who perches on a fallen branch in shade,
Lifting one tilted hinge
Lopsidedly as if recalling
Long noiseless swoops from barn to barn
When he was still a menacing shadow.
He accepts the rat
With dignity, his intact eye
An awful inquiry
Fixing ours. The third lid shutters, opaque,
Back and forth over the blasted one,
A yellow map of jagged black islands.
He puffs up big at our approach
But doesn't flee. He is the predator.

IV

The colt sprawls in the sun
In a dome of flies.
Sudden violent twistings, then
Collapse. His huge dark eye,
Moist as a grape, rolls
In terror. His cries
Are silent ones. Just weaned, he's learned
The hopelessness of bawling.
You give him morphine. He doesn't
Want to die, this feisty little one,
Staggering to his tiny hoofs to thrust
His muzzle into water, come up dripping,
Not swallowing, his eyes
Terribly hurt, then down, rolling again,
Learning how to stop living
In the agony of a twisted gut.

V

The backhoe comes to dig him under.
In the far field, mares in foal
Are grazing, and the August sky,
Shorn of clouds, bloats bright blue,
Brash as the barn man with his red muscles
And unblinking pleasant bovine stare.

VI

The owl waits for the long day
To cripple into nightfall.
He won't make it
Either, eyeshot, equilibrium
Vanquished. He ruffles himself
To the largest version of threat he can
And postures furiously against tomorrow.

Acknowledgments

Grateful acknowledgment is made to the following publications in which poems in this collection first appeared, some in earlier versions:

Abbey: "Pederson's"
Albatross: "Drought"
Backstreet: "March 24"
Broadkill Review: "Ox Team at Garfield Farm"
Chiron Review: "Farming," "Hayhook," "Fences"
Gargoyle: "Barn Fire"
George State University Review: "Dead Horses"
Icon: "Western Minnesota"
Iodine: "Renovations"
Nimrod: "Hammering"
North American Review: "The Lunar Year"
Quest: "Witch"
the new renaissance: "Heartless," "Founder," "Two Deaths," "Requiem for a Farrier"
Tipton Poetry Journal: "Country Burial," "Saddlesoap"
Wilderness House: "The Threshing Bee and Steam Show"

Cover art, "morning," by Gabriella Fabbri (duchesssa on sxc.hu); photo of the author by Alan Colby; cover and interior design by Diane Kistner (dkistner@futurecycle.org); Trebuchet MS interior text with Engebrechtre titling

About FutureCycle Press

FutureCycle Press is dedicated to publishing lasting English-language poetry and flash fiction books, chapbooks, and anthologies in both print-on-demand and ebook formats. Founded in 2007 by long-time independent editor/publishers and partners Diane Kistner and Robert S. King, the press incorporated as a nonprofit in 2012. A number of our editors are distinguished poets and authors in their own right, and we have been actively involved in the small press movement going back to the early seventies.

Our annual anthology, *FutureCycle*, combines poetry and flash fiction. The FutureCycle Poetry Book Prize and honorarium is awarded annually for the best full-length volume of poetry we publish in a calendar year. We are dedicated to giving all authors we publish the care their work deserves, making our catalog of titles the most distinguished it can be, and paying forward any earnings to fund more great books.

We've learned a few things about independent publishing over the years. We've also evolved a unique, resilient publishing model that allows us to focus mainly on vetting and preserving for posterity the most books of exceptional quality without becoming overwhelmed with bookkeeping and mailing, fundraising activities, or taxing editorial and production "bubbles." To find out more about what we are doing, come see us at www.futurecycle.org.

www.ingramcontent.com/pod-product-compliance
Lightning Source LLC
LaVergne TN
LVHW051806080426
835511LV00019B/3421